First Facts™

Our Physical World

Energy

by Christine Webster

Consultant:
Philip W. Hammer, PhD
Vice President, The Franklin Center
The Franklin Institute
Philadelphia, Pennsylvania

Capstone
press

Mankato, Minnesota

First Facts is published by Capstone Press
151 Good Counsel Drive, P.O. Box 669, Mankato, Minnesota 56002
www.capstonepress.com

Library of Congress Cataloging-in-Publication Data
Webster, Christine.
    Energy / by Christine Webster.
    p. cm.—(First facts. Our physical world)
    Includes bibliographical references and index.
    Contents: Energy—Energy forms—Changing energy—Potential and kinetic energy—Energy
from the sun—Energy to electricity—James Prescott Joule—Sun safety—Amazing but true!—
Hands on: saving energy.
    ISBN 0-7368-2616-5 (hardcover)
    1. Power resources—Juvenile literature. 2. Power (Mechanics)—Juvenile literature. [1. Power
resources. 2. Power (Mechanics)] I. Title. II. Series.
TJ163.23.W39 2005
621.042—dc22
    2003027406

Summary: Introduces energy and provides instructions for an activity to demonstrate
    some of its characteristics.

Editorial Credits
Christopher Harbo, editor; Linda Clavel, series designer; Molly Nei, book designer;
    Scott Thoms, photo researcher; Eric Kudalis, product planning editor

Photo Credits
Capstone Press/Gary Sundermeyer, cover, 10, 11
Comstock, 9
Dwight R. Kuhn, 12
Folio Inc./Richard Cummins, 6–7; Tom McCarthy, 5
Getty Images Inc./AFP, 8; Sean Gallup, 13
Index Stock Imagery/Buck Lovell, 4; Dave Rusk, 14–15
Mary Evans Picture Library, 17
PhotoDisc Inc., 20
SuperStock/Nathan Michaels, 18–19

1 2 3 4 5 6 09 08 07 06 05 04

Table of Contents

Energy

Energy gives things the ability to move or do work. A train uses energy to pull cars along a track. A TV uses energy to make pictures and sounds.

People need energy to live and grow. They get energy from the food they eat. People use energy to work, play, and think.

Energy Forms

Every day, people use many forms of energy. Light energy helps plants grow. Heat energy warms homes. **Mechanical energy** moves cars and machines. Electricity is energy that lights buildings and streets at night.

Fun Fact! Sunlight travels from the sun to earth in about 8 minutes.

7

Changing Energy

Energy changes form. A car engine turns the **chemical energy** in gasoline into mechanical energy. The engine turns the wheels.

The telephone turns sound energy into electricity. The electricity passes through a wire. Another telephone turns the electricity back into sound.

Potential and Kinetic Energy

Potential energy is stored energy.
It does nothing. But it can change into
another form. A ball has potential
energy when it is held.

Kinetic energy is the energy of motion. People have kinetic energy when they run. A ball has kinetic energy when it is bounced.

Energy from the Sun

Most energy on earth comes from the sun. Sunlight gives plants energy to live and grow. Plants use sunlight to change air and water into food.

Dead plants become **fuels** that people use. Coal is made from plants that died millions of years ago. People burn coal for energy.

14

Energy to Electricity

People make machines to turn energy into electricity. Water behind a dam has potential energy. Inside some dams, machines change the kinetic energy of falling water into electricity. The electricity lights and heats homes and businesses.

Fun Fact!
Most of the electricity used in the United States is made by burning coal.

James Prescott Joule

James Prescott Joule was an English scientist. He studied what things are made of and how they work. Joule helped discover a **law** about saving energy. He found that energy used in one form always changes into another form. Energy is never lost.

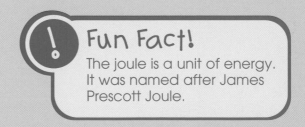

Fun Fact!
The joule is a unit of energy. It was named after James Prescott Joule.

T′   T

C′

S′

S

C

17

Sun Safety

Energy from the sun can burn skin. People need to protect their skin from the sun's harmful rays. They should wear sunscreen while outside.

Lightning is a form of electrical energy. It forms when electricity builds up in the sky. Lightning can travel 90,000 miles (145,000 kilometers) per second. It has enough energy to light a 100-watt lightbulb for three months.

Hands On: Saving Energy

People use insulation to help keep their homes warm in the winter. You can see how adding layers of insulation helps save heat energy. Ask an adult to help you with this activity.

What You Need

scissors
2 plastic cup lids
2 thermometers

water
4 foam cups

What You Do

1. Use a scissors to cut a small hole in the center of each plastic cup lid. Make each hole big enough for a thermometer to fit through.
2. Turn on the hot water faucet. Let the water get hot.
3. Fill one cup half full of hot water. Be careful as you fill the cup because the water may be very hot.
4. Fill a second cup half full of hot water. Stack this cup inside the two remaining cups.
5. Carefully put the plastic lids on the cups of water. Slide the thermometers into the holes in the lids.
6. Wait 20 minutes. Check the temperatures of the cups. Which cup has the hotter water?

The set of three cups should have kept its water warmer longer. It had three layers of foam to hold in the heat energy.

Glossary

chemical energy (KEM-uh-kuhl EN-ur-jee)—the energy of a substance that is released through a chemical reaction

fuel (FYOO-uhl)—a source of energy; coal, oil, and natural gas are fuels.

kinetic energy (ki-NET-ik EN-ur-jee)—the energy of a moving object

law (LAW)—a statement in science about what always happens when certain events take place

mechanical energy (muh-KAN-uh-kuhl EN-ur-jee)—the energy an object has because of its motion or position

potential energy (puh-TEN-shuhl EN-ur-jee)—the stored energy of an object that is raised, stretched, or squeezed

Read More

Bradley, Kimberly Brubaker. *Energy Makes Things Happen.* Let's-Read-And-Find-Out Science. New York: HarperCollins, 2003.

Farndon, John. *Energy.* Science Experiments. Tarrytown, N.Y.: Benchmark Books, 2003.

Stille, Darlene R. *Energy: Heat, Light, and Food.* Amazing Science. Minneapolis: Picture Window Books, 2004.

Internet Sites

FactHound offers a safe, fun way to find Internet sites related to this book. All of the sites on FactHound have been researched by our staff.

Here's how:

1. Visit *www.facthound.com*
2. Type in this special code **0736826165** for age-appropriate sites. Or enter a search word related to this book for a more general search.
3. Click on the **Fetch It** button.

FactHound will fetch the best sites for you!

Index